THE DIAGNOSTIC MANUAL OF MISHEGAS

DMOM

Potchkied together and .com-piled by

Jay Neugeboren
Michael B. Friedman
Lloyd I. Sederer M.D.

ISBN-10: 1483994740
EAN-13: 9781483994741

Library of Congress Control Number: 2013906513
CreateSpace Independent Publishing Platform
North Charleston, South Carolina

THE DIAGNOSTIC
MANUAL OF
MISHEGAS

DMOM

Potchkied together and .com-piled by

Jay Neugeboren
Michael B. Friedman
Lloyd I. Sederer M.D.

Based upon a newly discovered document
by the brilliant if frequently famisht

Dr. Sol Farblondget, M.D., Ph.D., P.T.A.

*"All men and women are meshugah, but some
men and women are more meshugah than others."*

— Gershem Orwell. *Funny Farm.*

THE DIAGNOSTIC MANUAL OF MISHEGAS

Table of Contents

How the Diagnostic Manual of Mishegas—our D.M.O.M.—came to be!

So how, you are asking, did this wonderfully utilitarian, totally *fartoots* (discombobulated), often splendidly incomprehensible classic of irreverence, indulgence, and pure, unadulterated *seychel* (wisdom) come to be?

And the answer: How do you think it came to be?

It came to be because the renowned physician and acclaimed Yiddish scholar, Doctor Sol Farblondget, after his daily breakfast of bagels, onions, lox, onions, smoked whitefish, onions, sable, onions, cream cheese, onions, pickled herring, onions, creamed herring, onions, sour pickles, and a glass hot tea, decided, on a whim and a prayer (and a major early morning attack of flatulence), to bring into being new and better ways to comprehend what it means to be *mishugah.*

And how did he do it?

By cooking with gas (much of which he created himself), as he recently told us in his inimical and sometimes *farshtinkener* way —and after witnessing his weary colleagues struggle to produce yet another version of their highly successful, internally *ferkacht*, and often unintelligable thousand page so-called "Bible of Psychiatry," the *D.S.M.* (*The Diagnostic and Statistical Manual of Psychiatric Disorders*)—he was inspired to create a simple, sensible, and wonderfully fanciful alternative.

And what did we do with Doctor Farblondget's bizarre, shrewd, and thoroughly perplexing scribblings, books, and essays?

We used them to create *The Diagnostic Manual of Mishegas*, which will enable readers to transform ordinary *tsuris* and *mishegas*—the glooms, blues, *angsts*, and general *chazzerei* of their lives, heretofore catalogued by the *D.S.M.* and its global counterpart the *ICD*—into transcendent and easy-to-understand categories. Through treatment modalities— something found nowhere in the *D.S.M.*—that will transform *kvetching* into *kvelling* and *guilt* into *gelt*[1]* —

---

1 * For a heartwarming how-to guide that surpasses Horatio Alger Jr.'s *From Rags to Riches* in its wise whimsicality, and explains how to take advantage of the guilt of others while

we enable readers to learn to live at peace with their inner *mishegas*, and to treasure its precious, absurd, and life-giving looniness.

But first, the tale of how one heroic *mishugener* helped bring us to our better selves — so that instead of forever *shlepping* around real but useless feelings and *tsuris* we intended to shove down the garbage disposal of our lives years ago, we can regain the ability to *shep nachas* and be *froelich*, because we are once again alive to the wonder and insanity of life's *cockamamy* quirks, curiosities, and *mishegas*.

---

selling off your own guilt at antique shows, on e-bay, and at tag sales, see Sol Farblondget's soul-stirring *The Joy of Guilt*.

The Story of
How the D.M.O.M. Came to Be

"The controversies about the revisions [of the D.S.M.] have highlighted the influence of the manual, which brings in more than $5 million annually to the association and is written by a group of 162 specialists in relative secrecy. Besieged from all sides, the association has received about 25,000 comments on the proposed changes from treatment centers, hospital representatives, government agencies, advocates for patient groups and researchers. The organization has declined to make these comments public."

— **"D.S.M. REVISIONS MAY SHARPLY INCREASE ADDICTIONS."**
The New York Times

"A Selective Serotonin Re-Uptake Inhibitor is no substitute for a good piece herring."

— *The Diagnostic Manual of Mishegas.*

At 8:32 P.M. on a cold, rainy, mid-summer night, Doctor Sol Farblondget (M.D., Ph. D., P.T.A.), entered a crumbling east side brownstone where a clandestine sub-committee of the American Psychiatric Association was inventing new psychiatric disorders they intended to add to the hundreds of disorders already listed in the 943 page fourth edition of the *D.S.M. – The Diagnostic and Statistical Manual of Psychiatric Disorders*. In addition to being a brilliant psychiatrist, Sol Farblondget was a lifelong lover of the Yiddish language, which for him, especially as it pertained to the abiding *mishegas* of life, reflected the accumulated wisdom of the Jewish people through the ages.

Having donned a disguise in an abandoned phone booth—a moustache drawn with black magic marker, dark horn-rimmed glasses, a sombrero, a serape draped over his left shoulder, and an unlit cigar stub lightly pasted to his lower lip—Sol made his way into the brownstone's vestibule, where he was stopped by a security guard sucking a Sherlock Holmes-style briar-and-porcelain pipe.

"Who are you, and would you like to tell me why you've come here this evening?" the guard asked.

I'm Gaucho Marx," Sol replied, "and I'm here to talk to a shrink."

"Aha—a shrink rap! Of course," the guard said. "But do you belong to our club?"

"I don't care to belong to any club that will have me as a member," Sol said.

"I feel for your ambivalence," the security guard said, and he held Sol in a long embrace before wishing him a safe journey and generous third party reimbursements.

Minutes later, Sol entered a fifth-floor room littered with empty designer water bottles, its air reeking of cigar smoke, shameful desires, and repressed memories. On two sides of a long table, ten psychiatrists were napping in stress-free lounge chairs beside couches devoid of patients while at the far end of the room a bearded man and a woman in an Armani pants suit were lying head-to-toe on adjoining couches, and debating the relationship between disordered pecking orders and disordered peckers .

Sol stamped his L.L. Bean all-season galoshes, flamenco-style, thereby waking all but six of the psychiatrists.

"Revolution time, my friends," he announced.

"Time to vote on a resolution?" asked one of the waking psychiatrists. "I vote yes, but with exceptions for psychopathological conditions not otherwise specified."

"Take off the funny clothes, and get out of here, Sol," said Doctor Herbert Luftmensch, chairman of the sub-committee. "We already got more input than we can turn into output."

Sol whipped out a thin sheaf of papers from under his sombrero. "I'm here with the answer to your prayers, Herb," he said. "A miracle manual that the whole world will be able to understand, unlike the Bible of our field, which is an over-priced doorstopper of a book no one can understand even after a gezillion years of psychoanalysis, cognitive behavioral therapy, and pharmaceutical company junkets to beautiful Carribean islands."

"Aren't you Sol Farblondget—author of *Strudel and its Relation to the Unconscious*?" a psychiatrist asked.

"And editor of the Irish-Jewish classic, *The Book of Kvells*?" asked another.

"And let's not forget my best-selling and shamelessly self-absorbed *I'm OK — You're Totally Mishugah*, a book I conceived while sunning myself atop the Yenne Velt Landfill on Staten Island—the very place where early this morning I came up with my most compassionately brilliant *k'nocker* of an idea yet."

"So whatcha got, Pops?" asked Morris Milchadig, who had once served as Chief Tummler at Saturday night fun-raising Blintz-Booze-and-Barf Blow-Outs ("Let it all out in a safe, non-intimate environment") for Sol's renegade splinter group M.O.M. (*Mayvens of Mishegas, L.L.P.*, their motto: *'We love our M.O.M.!'*). "But what's with the L.L.P.—have you and your team gone corporate?"

"L.L.P. serves as a Shakespearian reminder of the common humanity we share when lost on the ever-changing border between madness, sanity, and the South Jersey Shore," Sol said, and began reciting lines his organization used to open their ill-attended triennial meetings: "The Lunatic, the Lover, and the Poet are of imagination all compact . . . . "

"*Enough!*" Herbert Luftmensch said. "Your inflection is wrong, and what's more, Shakespeare never used capital letters."

Unflustered by such brusque disdain, Sol addressed his colleagues. "What I got here — *The Diagnostic Manual of Mishegas* — is an ingenious alternative to your *D.S.M.*, and to all the *fershlugenah* therapies that flow from its unfathomable run-on sentences," he said. "Hey — let's face it, guys, we're *all* a little *mishugah*, right? So what I do here is to simplify the whole *shmeer* by dividing the world into two groups — those who suffer from *mishegas major* . . . and those who suffer from *mishegas minor*."

"Not so fast, Farblondget," said Andrews Crotch-Morgan, the lone non-Jewish member of the A.P.A.'s covert work-group. "Does your system pay due attention to exhaustive phenomenological sub-groups and sub-types along with samplings of the multitude of contradictory course specifiers that allow for evaluating diagnostic criteria and employing appropriate numerical codes to them and to their alternate code numbers (necessarily enclosed in parentheses), allowing for clarification of pertinent Factitious, Dissociative, and Appendix-related Disorders that are rarely if ever wholly relevant ?"

"You got it," Sol said. "So when I use the the term *mishegas major* I'm talking about people who are *really, really mishugah* — for example, a person who talks with God without first getting permission from his Rabbi, priest, or health insurance provider. And by *mishegas minor*, I'm talking about everyone else—for instance, an *alter kocker* who believes his beautiful, brilliant, sexually voracious young wife when she tells him she is going to love him forever."

Doctor Emanuel Bulbenick raised his hand. "Does being sexually voracious qualify as an eating disorder?" he asked.

"Is it covered by Medicare?" asked Doctor Shimmel Dreckstein. "And what about pharmaceutical companies? If we don't play patty-cake with them, where will we get our pocket protectors and ball point pens?"

"Consider my visit a peace offering," Sol responded. "Keep your *D.S.M.*, but add the *D.M.O.M.*! Let's unite, throw off our non-profitable categories, and make *everyone* a potential patient! Because while your *D.S.M.* makes distinctions between thousands of conditions few people have experienced and nobody can understand, it doesn't say a word about the *mishegas-of-everyday-life* and *what-to-do-about-it!* It never even mentions, for example, the healing powers of food, drink, travel, and sex, which can provide our clients with pleasures that go beyond the wellness principle.

"Let me give you some for-instances," Sol continued. "For people suffering from *mishegas major*, especially those living in mental hospitals or locked psychiatric wards, the cost can come to well more than a thousand dollars a day. But a two-week vacation in Paris or Tuscany in the spring, or the Caribbean or South America in winter, in the company of a C.D.M.O.M.T. (Certified D.M.O.M.

Therapist) *and* live-in gourmet cook, comes to less than half that amount, including taxes and baggage fees.

"And when it comes to most varieties of *mishegas minor*, a hot corned beef sandwich on rye, followed by a full body massage with a happy ending and a sexually enhanced night of sleep—or a large tumbler of a favorite alcoholic libation imbibed while watching a movie featuring Buster Keaton, Charlie Chaplin, Bob Hope, Oscar Levant, or—most favored nation of all—the Marx Brothers. And for feelings that arise from the ordinary *tsuris* of life, such as losing a job, being called for jury duty, or getting stuck in the Holland Tunnel on a hot summer day when your air conditioner has gone kaput, a walk in a sylvan setting with your sweetheart, or someone else's, will do wonders."

"But the *D.S.M.* has earned our organization more than one hundred million dollars!" Doctor Mazumagrubber objected. "So if there's no *D.S.M.* and no *D.S.M.* codes, how will we make a living? What about our royalties?"

"You don't understand," Sol said. "You can *keep* your D.S.M. and your royalties. But by publishing the *D.M.O.M.* for a mere $10 a pop, we can rake in additional millions. Next we offer regionally marketed editions, with ads from travel agencies, dating services, cruise companies, luxury spas, fantasy baseball camps, and beer, wine, and booze companies. So whaddaya think—bury the hatchet, or use it to keep hacking at the frozen sea within?"

Herbert Luftmensch banged his fist on the table, and said that he voted 'No!' to any book that was so short, clear, and simple that *anyone* could understand it. If Farblondget's book were published, who would ever need therapy again, much less the *D.S.M.*? Tillie Eulenspiegel, who had been head-to-toe with Clarkson Scott-Goldberg III, now stood and praised Farblondget and his manual. Luftmensch called the question, and the vote of members who were not asleep was three to two in favor of Luftmensch's motion, whereupon Eulenspiegel and Scott-Goldberg III marched Sol around the the table chanting "Long live the *Manual of Mishegas!*" at which point Luftmensch had Sol dragged from the room and pushed down the stairs where the briar-and-porcelain pipe-smoking guard asked if he would like to a) share the experience with him, b) have him call an ambulance, or 3) pre-order a copy of the newly revised 1000 page *D.S.M.*.

"Never never never never never," Sol said, "because I'm nothing if not lear-y . . . "

Which was when we arrived, and Sol told us his story.

"*Mazel Tov!*" we cried. "*Alevai!*" we shouted. "*Shehechayanu!*" we sang. And there and then we agreed to start *potchkieing* together and to publish the *D.M.O.M.*.

The Diagnostic Manual
Of Mishegas

Introduction: How Diagnostic Criteria Are Organized

Organized?! Who are we kidding? This book — *boruch hashem* and *hallelujah!* — is splendidly *dis*organized. If you want 'organized,' you're reading the wrong book. But if you want wisdom, laughs, and astonishing insights into just how *mishugah* life can be — if you want to learn how to cope with *mishegas* and glory in it, then read on! Because what we have here are diagnostic categories — cannily *ongepotchket* (slapped together creatively, as in a Rube Goldberg contraption), and arranged according to Doctor Sol Farblondget's cunning *reductio ad absurdum* (and when we say *absurdum,* we ain't just talking) that reduces the *mishegas* of this world into two major categories: *Mishegas Major* . . . and *Mishegas Minor.*

Mishegas Major: As Sol explained to the *shmendricks* who were working on the *D.S.M., mishegas major* refers to someone who is *really, really mishugah* — for example, a man who, persuaded by his doctor that he is not a chicken, continues to lay eggs.

Mishegas Minor: This category refers to most of us most of the time. We're all a little *mishugah*, right? For example, a young woman who worries because the young man she is engaged to is more excited by a New York Knicks victory than oral sex.

Some ethnic and religious groups, such as Jews, Puerto Ricans, Italians, and SCLIFs (Senior Citzens Living in Florida) love dwelling on their *mishegas* (as in familiar conversational tropes such as "You think *your* mother-in-law is *mishugah*? Ha! Wait till you meet mine!"). Others, such as WASPs — the *mishegoyim* — insist on giving highest priority and value not only to non-expression of feelings and to an insistence on buying retail, but to tight lips and tighter asses (for an analysis of this phenomenon, see Sol Farblondget's seminal paper, "The Riddle of the Sphincter: WASPS, Sexual Inhibition, and Bowel Retention").

Cultural variations complicate diagnosis, and differences between *mishegas major* and *mishegas minor* may not always be clear. A for-instance: Is a man alone in a car, and hearing voices, having an attack of *mishegas major* or *mishegas minor* if he keeps shouting to the empty seat next to him: "I told you a thousand times, Esther — I know which way to turn to get onto the Merritt Parkway, so stop *hocking* (nagging) me already!" And does the diagnosis depend upon the hearing of voices, familiar or imagined (as in: "Now listen to me, God, you sadistic *momzer* — if you tell me one more time that 'Yes, my child, bad things happen to good people, and this too shall pass,' I'll drive this car right through your pearly gates with Esther lashed to the hood!"), or on whether or not the voices enable him to make the correct turns?

Categories Of Mishegas

1.0 Nervous Conditions Of Everyday Life

Nervous conditions are part of the human condition, and thus are as different in their variations as human beings are different from one another. Still, it is helpful to understand what *form* of nervousness you are experiencing, or what type of *tsuris*-addict is torturing you with tales of woe, and to thereby figure out how to tell the feeling, or the person, to *gei avek* (get lost!), *gei shluffen* (go to sleep), or — our number one suggestion, especially when the meter is running out on your patience for listening to yet another mournful *Oy Vey*-drenched soliloquy — to tell the *tsuris*-addict to *fardrai zich deyn kopf* (literally: 'Go turn your own head around' — i.e., to leave me alone and make yourself nuts!) Also: a good hot pastrami sandwich, don't skimp on the mustard, with a nice, fat sour pickle on the side, can't hurt.

Sol Farblondget, in his talks to gatherings of 'The *Mayvens* of *Mishegas*,' liked to point out the particularly evocative quality of Yiddish (deriving as it does from thousands of years of direct experience of *tsuris*), when dealing with various forms of *mishegas*. Yiddish is also a time-saver. For example, to ask a patient who comes to your office if he or she is feeling troubled or confused, as the *D.S.M.* would have it, usually results in an answer something like, "Oh yes, doctor. I feel troubled and confused," to which the doctor will reply, "Would you like to tell me more?" — to which patients usually reply, "Not really," or "Do I have to?"

Compare this to asking someone who comes for a consultation, "Are you feeling maybe a little *farmisht*, or is it more like maybe being *farfolen*?" to which the typical response will be something like, "*Farmisht* is *exactly* the way I've been feeling, doctor, and let me tell you why . . . . "

Here follow a list of common nervous conditions that, though different in kind, one from the other, have many qualities in common and, depending on a particular day's Dow Jones Industrial Average or the state of your *kishkas* (intestines), can sometimes be used interchangeably.

1.01 Tsuris Reactions and Sequelae

Although Jews like to claim a monopoly on *tsuris*, the truth is that this condition (troubles, aggravation, worries, suffering) befalls everyone, and most of what passes for *mishegas* is a natural reaction to life's vagaries and pitfalls. Thus, when a 54 year old woman becomes depressed because her accountant husband, also 54, has taken up with an 18 year old hotsie-totsie, she is not *mishugah* and in need of psychotropic medications. What she needs, we believe, is to shack up with an 18 year old lifeguard or tennis pro, and to leave her husband a note, informing him that as an accountant he should realize that 18 can go into 54 many more times than 54 can go into 18.

As Sol Farblondget has wisely noted, the point is not to moan, groan, and carry on about the *tsuris* that has befallen you, *but to do something about it.* Remember: when the Children of Israel fled from Egypt and came to the Red Sea with the Egyptians in hot pursuit, and they complained to God that he had delivered them from slavery into something worse than slavery, and Moses, who did not even ask for a retainer, went to God on their behalf and transmitted his tribe's complaints, God laughed. "Wherefore criest thou unto me?" God said. "Go forth!" And it was only when the Children of Israel stopped *kvetching,* and plunged forward into the Red Sea, that the waters parted.

1.02 Tsuris-addiction

Tsuris-addiction is a wide-spread condition which, by cutting people off from their innate capacity for pleasure and encouraging *kvetching* (complaining), enables them to spread *gevalt*-laden gloom and doom everywhere. In an iconic example, four elderly Jewish women are wading ankle-deep in the waters at Brighton Beach. "*Oy*," says Ethel. "*Oy vey*," says Molly. "*Oy vey iz mir*," says Lillie. "Please, ladies," says Annie. "We promised not to talk about our children."

People who have life-long love affairs with, and attachments to, misery, wind up living in what we think of as *The Village of Oy Vey Iz Mir* at whose center is the *Shtiebel* of *Gornish Helfin*. *Tsuris*-addicts spend their lives holding on to every morsel of real or imagined bad news they ever had—*kvetching*, for example, about how unfair it is that they had to grow up near people with bigger houses, better time-shares, more cashmere sweaters, and fancier cabanas than theirs. In *Oy Vey Iz Mir*, any and every event is cause for weeping and wailing. Thus, a woman afflicted with this condition on a transcontinental train will cry out every few minutes, "*Oh, do I have a headache . . . Oh, do I have a headache . . . !*" until a nice young man in a nearby sleeper compartment, kept awake by her moaning, puts on his pajama top and slippers, goes to the woman's sleeper, tells her he has heard her cry, and has brought her two aspirin. The woman thanks him, takes the aspirin, and goes back to sleep. The man returns to his sleeper, and for three minutes all is well. Then from the woman's sleeper, a new lament: "*Oh did I have a headache . . . Oh, did I have a headache . . . !*"

That '*tsuris*-addiction' is a regrettable and an oft-considered natural part of life is not even mentioned in the *D.S.M.* (Nor is '*tsuris*-attachment,' which is pretty much the same thing, except that you can send it to someone in an e-mail.) While some studies show that *tsuris*-addicts may take what they consider genuine (if perverse) pleasure from being miserable, the price of their pleasure is often to plunge many of us into a desire to rip out their vocal cords.

There are those individuals, however, who, benefiting from the wisdom of Sol Farblondget, have learned to take comfort from the *tsuris* of others.

For example, Sammy and Shlomo meet on the boardwalk in Atlantic City after not having seen one another for many years,

"So how are you?" Sammy asks.

"Not so good," Shlomo answers. "Maybe you heard, maybe not—but my partner stole all my money?"

"That's terrible," Sammy says. "But it could be worse."

"Actually, it is worse. My wife, the love of my life, ran off with my partner *and* my money."

"That's terrible," Sammy says. "But it could be worse."

"Well, to tell the truth, it is worse," Shlomo says. "My son, the hope of my life, dove into an empty swimming pool, and now he's brain-damaged for the rest of his life."

"That *is* terrible," Sammy says. "But it could be worse."

"What do you mean it could be worse?" Shlomo asks angrily. "I've lost my money, my wife, and my son. How could it be worse?"

"It could have happened to me," says Sammy.

17

1.02A: The Wisdom of Gornish Helfin

Although the *D.S.M.* makes a big deal out of *attachment* theory, we are advocates of *de*-tachment theory, since experience convinces us that what proves most helpful both to those addicted to *tsuris*, and those who must suffer from relationships with *tsuris*-addicts, is the concept of *Gornish Helfin* (meaning, literally, "Nothing will help"), which concept can be explained by the following archetypal example.

When the great Yiddish actor Mendel Kupietzky fell down *kerplunk!* in the middle of a Yiddish-language performance of *King Lear*, and a doctor rushed to the stage and began examining him, a man in the balcony started yelling, "*Give him an enema. . . . ! Give him an enema. . . . !*" And when, a moment later, the doctor threw out his hands in a gesture of helplessness, and announced that Mendel Kupietzky was dead — still the man from the balcony kept yelling "*Give him an enema . . . ! Give him an enema. . . . !*" and would not stop despite pleas from other actors and members of the audience. Only when the theater manager appeared alongside the doctor and looked up at the man in the balcony and said, "He's dead, sir. An enema can't help. *Gornish Helfin . . . Gornish Helfin . . .*" — only then did the man in the balcony change his tune. "*Give him an enema!*" he cried one last time. "*It can't hurt . . . .*"

Once we understand that no matter what we do to and for some people, they will not change — that *Gornish Helfin* (or "*GH*" as Sol Farblondget liked to acronymize it), and therefore the best thing is to *leave-them-be* — we free ourselves from the quintessential American illusion, pragmatic to its core, that there is no problem for which there is not a happy solution. What we believe is that for many situations and conditions, including most forms of *mishegas* — '*tsuris*-addiction' at the top of the list — *there is nothing to be done*.[1] Thus, *any* engagement with the *tsuris*-addict — especially telling the addict that *kvetching* about *tsuris* is not such a hot idea — merely brings on ever-rising levels of *tsuris*-addiction.

For *tsuris*-addicts, *insatiability* is the name of the game. Nothing will ever please them, and it is a waste of time — truly *mishugah*! — to point out that they have no *real* reasons for being miserable, or to urge them to find ways to be happy. [2]

---

1 'There is nothing to be done' may overstate the case, for with *tsuris*-addiction, as with all forms of *mishegas*, we agree with Sol Farblondget that a good meal, a nice glass wine, a massage, a nap, a stroll in a beautiful setting with a friend, a hefty income tax refund, and/or an afternoon or night of love (all electronic devices turned off) can't hurt — and may even encourage pleasure to move in where *tsuris* and sorrow previously reigned.

2 There is a voluminous literature about the seemingly genetic inability of some people, notably WASPs — the *mishegoyim* — to experience happiness. For the *mishegoyim*, as Erik Erickson has noted, due to their "restricted modes of feeling," it is not so much that they court misery but that *they distrust feeling good*, much less being capable of happiness, bliss, or hunky-doriness, and have come, effectively, to regard happiness as itself a form of *mishegas*. For a more extended commentary on the subject, which may prove something of a downer to our sybaritcally-oriented friends, see Sol Farblondget's essay "Happiness and its Discontents."

Thus, in a well-known, mega-analyzed example, a mother sends her son two silk ties for his birthday, and when the son appears at her door for his birthday dinner wearing one of the ties, the mother is immediately distraught. "So what's the matter," she says. "You didn't like the *other* tie?"

"There is no *dayenu* in these people's lives," Sol Farblondget has often said, meaning—as in the song from the Passover Seder, where for each miracle God performed for us, we chant "*Dayenu:* it would have been enough had He done nothing else"—that some people are never satisfied. If you understand this, Sol believes, and let *de*-tachment theory work for you, you can learn to lower expectations, and not drive yourself *mishugah* by hoping for change where change is unlikely to occur. Therefore, when engaged in relationships with *tsuris*-addicts, and you sense an impulse to enter into dialogue with them, the suggestion here is to cock your head to the side, furrow your brow in feigned sympathy, and stare through or past the addict while silently repeating, "*Gornish helfin . . . Gornish helfin . . . Gornish helfin . . .* " This way, if by some miracle these people ever do change, you have not destroyed whatever good will may exist between you, and they remain ready to embrace you.

1.03 Verklempt.

Being *verklempt* is characterized by a profound sense of bitter disappointment and sadness, often accompanied by a feeling of having been wronged. Although both men and women can be, and often are, *verklempt*, women are far more likely to be *openly verklempt*, frequently grabbing their breasts and wailing, "I am *verklempt*! Oh am I *verklempt*!" For example: "Can you believe it? I found the perfect man for my daughter — a doctor, handsome, from a good family. They dated. They went to a New England Country Inn on Lake Michigan for a couples weekend dedicated to 'Kosher Yoga and the Jewish Question.' They may even, *kein aina hara* ('there should be no evil eye') have had sex. And now she's gone and run off with a leather-jacketed *no-goodnick* on a motorcycle. I am *verklempt*."

Or a woman whose husband, as he rises from their bed on the morning of their 25th wedding anniversary, tells her that she is an ugly old hag — a *meiskeit* of *meiskeits* — and that never again will he feel obliged to sleep with her, or to look upon her repulsive face and body. "I am *verklempt*!' the woman will wail, and who can blame her? But to remain mired in *verklemptness* will serve only to drive her to more miserable conditions — to being *farmisht, farfolen, fartummelt, fartsadikt, ferdrayt, fershluggenah* (which terms we will define momentarily), and a ripe candidate for falling into the state of *Oy Vey Iz Mir*.

What the *D.M.O.M* recommends is that she telephone her husband in the early afternoon, and tell him she is still at home, and still in bed. And why is she still at home and in bed, he will ask (and if he doesn't, she raises the question), and what is her reply, guaranteed — especially when acted upon! — to relieve her feeling of being *verklempt*? "I'm in bed," she will tell him, "because I'm getting a second opinion."

1.04 Finster in di oygen.

Literally, 'darkness in one's eyes' — being on the verge of tears. For example, a nerd of a boy who is last to be chosen to the neighborhood ball team may get *finster in di oygen*, his tears magnified by the thickness of his eyeglasses. Or a wife who has been insulted by her husband, or a mother who despairs about her daughter's marital prospects, might cry out "I have *finster in di oygen*." But again, one can turn *finster in di oygen* to advantage. For example, a mother fearful that her son, if drafted, will die in combat the next morning, might recommend that he have *finster in di oygen* when he reads the eye-chart at his draft-board medical exam. This once happened to a young man we knew, who was given 4F status because of his poor eyesight. Later that day, when the young man was celebrating by going to the Angelica Theater in lower Manhattan to see a festival of silent movies, and was laughing away at Buster Keaton in 'The General,' he noticed that the man sitting next to him was the eye doctor who had examined him earlier in the day. "Excuse me," he said to the doctor, "but can you tell me if I'm on the right train for Newark, New Jersey?"

1.05 Tsimmis

A *tsimimis* is a bubbling pot of stewed fruit or vegetables, and 'to make a *tsimmis*' means to be so agitated that you can't stop making a fuss about your *tsuris* or your *nachas*. (*Nachas* = great joy, especially from the achievement of your child or grandchild; to *shep nachas* is to *get nachas* from your child or grandchild.) For example, a mother running along the beach and yelling, "Help! Help! My son the doctor is drowning!" Or Bella telling her friend, Blanche, that she has had *tsuris and nachas* from her son, Harvey. The *tsuris*? "Harvey is gay." The *nachas*? "The young man Harvey is living with is a doctor."

1.06 Plotz.

Plotzing is a literal falling down that mimics an inner emotional state, and though to *plotz* often represents a nervous condition that can express itself in physical symptoms and/or despairing lamentations—"What do you mean, don't make a *tsimmis* of it? I'm going to *plotz* already!"—it can also be utilized for states of well-being, as in: "My daughter took me to her new country club, and we played golf. Golf, she explained, was invented in her father-in-law's Slovakian *shtetl* when his *landsmen* earned their keep by clubbing small albino rodents to death and stuffing them down holes on wealthy landowners' estates. So when my daughter and I arrived at what they called 'the first greenie,' which every greenhorn from the *shtetl* would have crawled across in grateful wonder so verdantly manicured it was, and when I looked around at all the trees and lawns and ponds and cute little motorized wheelchairs, and thought 'O my America, my New-found-land of milk and *kugel!*', it was all so beautiful, I nearly *plotzed*."

1.07 Farmisht

A little confused and/or befuddled. For example, an elderly man walking along Collins Avenue in Miami Beach, stops another elderly man. "Listen," he asks, "was it you or your brother who died last week?"

1.08 Fartoots

Being discombobulated *and* bewildered. In the paradigmatic instance, a husband and wife meet with their rabbi because they have been having marital problems. The husband tells the rabbi he is *fartootsed* from all the demands his wife has been making on him. When he is finished talking, the rabbi says, "You know what? You're right." Then the wife tells the rabbi about how *fartootsed* she's becoming from the way her husband turns a deaf ear to all her reasonable requests.

"You know what?" the rabbi says. "You're right." "But darling," the *rebbetzin* (rabbi's wife) chimes in, "they can't *both* be right!" To which the rabbi says, "You know what? You're right too!"

1.09 Fartsadikt

More than a little confused and/or befuddled. For example, a man telephones the Kronkheit Psychiatric Institute and Nursing Home and asks for the Nurses' Station on the third floor. When he is connected, he asks if the nurse can call Milton Goldfarb to the phone. "I'm sorry to have to tell you this," the nurse says, "But Milton Goldfarb escaped from our home three hours ago."

"Thank God," the man replies. "Then I'm out."

1.10 Fartummelt

Confused and/or befuddled while also feeling that your head has been turned around, inside and out. For example, Hannah, standing in front of a Jackson Pollack painting at the Metropolitan Museum of Art, comments to her friend Mildred. "I like it, I like it—but it's so *ongepotchket* it makes me feel *fertummelt*."

1.11 Fardrayt

Confused, befuddled, *and* made dizzy. For example, a bride, on her wedding night, being told by her husband, as he gets into bed beside her, that he has had sexual relations with other men, so that the young woman, suddenly *ferdrayt*, doesn't know which way to turn.

1.12 Farfolen

A feeling of being 'lost' — not unlike what William James described as the 'oceanic feeling' at the heart of religious experience . . . except in an opposite direction. For instance, a very wealthy man we knew had a love-nest for his young sweetie-pie, whom he telephoned at 5:01 on a recent Tuesday to tell her that his board of directors had just met, and that in the morning he would hold a press conference and announce to the world that the multi-national corporation of which he was CEO was going belly up. "The ski lodge in Aspen, the Swiss bank accounts, the penthouse on Fifth Avenue, the round-the-world cruise, and everything else — gone, gone, all gone," he said. "But I'm calling you first thing before anyone else hears the news because the only thing that matters to me is if you will still love me."

"Of course, I'll still love you," his sweetie-pie said. And then, after a slight pause: "I'll *miss* you . . . "

Thus was the man *farfolen*.

1.13 Farshlugginah

The feeling of being beaten up by life. For example, Morris telling his friend Abe that he had a *fershlugginah* time the previous evening. "How so?" Abe asks. "Didn't you have tickets to go to the theater to see a translation into English of the great Yiddish play about those no-good children and how they made their father *fershlugginah* from the way they treated him?"

"I went to the play and it was terrific," Morris said. "But afterwards, I made the mistake of taking a shortcut through an alley for getting to the subway, and two men accosted me—a knife! a gun!—and told me to hand over my wallet, unbuckle my belt, let my pants down, count to thirty before moving, and that if I chased after them—ha! at my age, these wise alecks—they would do things to me I would regret. So I gave them my wallet, I let my pants down, and they ran off, and I was feeling even more *fershlugginah* than poor Mister Lear. I stood there in the alley, and I counted to thirty, and then— you know me, Abe—with my pants already down, and so that the experience wouldn't be a waste and I wouldn't go to sleep feeling totally *fershlugginah*, I peed against the wall."

1.14 Spilkes Minor and Spilkes Major

Spilkes is usually translated as having ants-in-the pants—a general state of being nervous and restless— but in its original and more comprehensive designation, it was *spilkes-in-tuchus (tuchus* = bottom, butt, rear-end). *Spilkes Major* and its step-child, *Spilkes Minor*, like *tsuris-addiction*, are among the most prevalent nervous disorders, and their intensity—whether we classify them as major or minor—is directly proportionate to major life events such as weddings, divorces, canasta tournaments, engagements, funerals, brisses, bar mitzvahs, packing for vacations, and long car rides when you have to pee badly and the next rest stop is more than 3.2 miles away. The classic example of *Spilkes* is of a Scotsman standing in front of a pay toilet. But more than frugality and one's bladder must be involved in serious and/or trivial instances of *Spilkes Major* and *Spilkes Minor*.

1.14.1 Spilkes Minor

The prevalence of *spilkes minor* cannot be overestimated and can be brought on by a multitude of ordinary events, many of them familial and intra-familial: meeting one's *mishpocheh* (in-laws) for the first time (or with the hope that the first time will be the last time); worrying that your grandson's admissions essay may not be good enough to get him accepted into a progressive Upper East Side play group; knowing with certainty that on the day of your child's second wedding, as happened on the first, the entire east coast will suffer a mid-summer power blackout and/or a record-breaking, mid-winter snow storm; being late for a date with the person you hope will ask you to marry him, when the conductor announces that due to a police incident, your Upper West Side Express train (#3) is being held in the station indefinitely, after which it will be re-routed directly to Trenton, New Jersey; or—more common, and often rising to the category of *spilkes major* — waiting, at the end of a brunch, luncheon, dinner, or family circle meeting, while your wife and her sisters and the *gantse mishphocheh* (the whole damned family, in-laws included) say their extended good-byes and begin to recount all the things they had meant to say to one another for which there has not been enough time, after which, in the car on the way home, you engage in a familiar and ritual shouting match with your wife in your ongoing *Who's-the-Bigger-Schmuck Debate* — you, for ever having married such a *yenta* (see: **Cockamamy Conditions of Character 2.10**), or your wife, for not having left you when she was still a size 8 and her dentist, Melvin Shvitzbud, with the most successful practice in The Five Towns, wanted to put more than fillings in her mouth and, for her other bodily orifices, all the gold and platinum she desired (which he could get at below cost).

1.14.2 Spilkes Major

Spilkes major is the most prevalent form of *mishegas major*, and Sol Farblondget provides an archetypal example: Moishe, at a railroad station in eastern Europe, sitting on a bench, head in hands, then standing and shaking his fists at the air, then sitting down and pacing the platform, bending forward every few steps, first in one direction and then in the other to see along the tracks, then once again sobbing and wailing away. When his friend, Yankel, sees him on the platform in a frenzied state, he hurries to him, and asks him what the problem is, at which question Moishe bursts into tears. A few minutes later, he calms down enough to reveal that he is so distraught because he missed his train, which left five minutes before.

"Oh," Yankel says, with a shrug. "From the way you were carrying on I thought you had missed it by an hour!"

Although the causes of *spilkes major* are often the same as the causes of *spilkes minor* and can themselves be either *major* (a dead car battery) or *minor* (the death of your mother-in-law), we differentiate *spilkes major* from *spilkes minor* by the extreme, sometimes hallucinatory behavior exhibited by the person afflicted. When one is afflicted with *spilkes major*, the *spilkes*—the nervousness, *angst*, ants-in-the-pants-and-*tuchus*—becomes a world unto itself.

A classic instance of *spilkes major*, which makes old-time categories such as *female hysteria* and the *D.T's* seem examples of normal human desires (for sex and drink), occurred on a dark and stormy night at the turn of this century. Doctor Herschel Minkowitz was holding evening office hours when suddenly he heard a ruckus in the waiting room, where Irving Abramowicz, a mild-mannered mortician who worked as a part-time customer service representative for the Internal Revenue Service, was being held back by two nurses.

"*I'm a moth, I'm a moth, I'm a moth!*" Irving was screaming at the top of his lungs. "I have to see the doctor. Let me *go*. Let me *go*! *I'm a moth, I'm a moth, I'm a moth . . . !*"

Doctor Minkowitz told the nurses to bring Irving into his office, where Irving kept repeating to the doctor that he was *certain* he was a moth, that he *knew* he was a moth, a moth, a moth . . .

Irving kept standing up and sitting down, flapping his arms wildly, turning in circles, sucking on window jambs, and attempting to squat on the leaves of house plants. Doctor Minkowitz tried to calm Irving down by assuring him that he was not, medically speaking, a moth.

"But I *am*, Doctor — I know it, I know it. I'm a moth . . . !"

"Well then," Doctor Minkowitz said, "since you're convinced you're a moth, Irving, I think the best thing for you to do is to see my psychiatrist colleague, Doctor Herbert Luftmensch."

At this point, Irving nodded vigorously. "Yes, yes," he said. "And I was on my way there . . . but the light was on in *your* office."

2.0 Cockamamy Conditions Of Character

Cockamamy (mixed-up in a colorful way; ridiculous; absurd) conditions of character/personality [3] include

---

[3] This category corresponds to what the *D.S.M.* misleadingly calls 'Personality Disorders," thereby creating undue embarrassment about conditions that for most of us are part of our ordinary *mishugener* ways of being, and usually not true and treatable medical conditions. For virtually all *cockamamy* conditions of character *gornisht helfen* is the operative diagnosis, though it can't hurt to try matzoh ball soup, a spa-day, a sitz

many varieties of being a *schmuck* (a jerk, dope, boob), such as being a *gantse schmuck* (a big jerk) or a *schmuck-with-earlaps* (a jerk who grew up in the Bronx) — or other ways of being part of a club you don't want to belong to: by being a *putz*, a *schlemiel*, a *schlemazel*, a *schemegegge*, a *schlub*, a *schnook*, a *yutz*, or a *schmendrik*. These are, for the most part, unchangeable character traits that no amount of money, therapy, drinking, or *hocking* (nagging) by others (mothers, wives, fiancés) can affect. (The same can be said about other *cockamamy* conditions of character: e.g., a *shnorrer*, a *momzer*, an *alrightnik*, a *noodj*, etc.)

Scientific surveys have shown, epidemiologically, endotontically, and epidermally,[3a] that according to the vast majority of women, *all* men are *schmucks* (with occasional exceptions for sons, grandsons, Spanish chefs, and Lebanese saxophone players). Conversely, though a woman may be seen by both men and women to have a variety of personality disorders (e.g., *yenta, kvetch, chalaria*), when it comes to character, women are infinitely superior to men) and are rarely if ever genuine *schmucks*. (See Sol Farblondget's classic text on marriage counseling: *Women on Top! Don't Stop Now!*)

Schmuck is also the yiddish word for penis, and as Sol Farblondget has insisted in his many articles on the subject (e.g., "Penis-Envy: Freud's Half-Cocked Delusions"), not only do women *not* want

---

bath, a cruise in the Bahamas, or playing hooky from work in the afternoon and going to a movie but not telling anyone you did.

3a Being *in-touch* with a *schmuck*.

to have this appendage hanging between their legs, but, being more skilful shoppers than men, they take pleasure from the variety of sensible substitutes available to them in Greenwich Village Sex Shops, online, and at out-of-town business conferences or Mah Jongg tournaments.

Thus, asked by her friend Doris, with whom she was traveling to an international marketing convention at a villa overlooking Lake Como, if she were meeting her husband there, Sheila replied, "When you go to a four star restaurant, do you bring a sandwich?"

Or a more telling example, taken from Sol's delightful *The World According to Schmucks*, there is the tale of Sheldon Schimmelpennick, who lost his penis in a car accident. When the surgeon, Doctor Nathan Shlong, visited with Sheldon and his wife, Irma, before Sheldon's discharge from the hospital, Doctor Shlong told Sheldon and Irma that thanks to remarkable technological breakthroughs, once Sheldon was fully healed, Doctor Shlong would be able to surgically append a fully functioning life-like penis to Sheldon's lower parts.

He then showed Sheldon and Irma detailed cutaway anatomical drawings of the potential new member that would replace Sheldon's lost cock, along with a price list. A standard-size new penis of about 5 to 6 inches (when fully aroused) would cost $10,000; a medium-size penis of 6 to 8 inches would cost $15,000, and—a Chanukah special extended until the new year—a 9 to 12 inch penis would be available at the bargain price of $17,500. Doctor

Shlong told Sheldon and Irma to take the brochure home, and inform him of their decision at their next post-operative consultation.

When, four weeks later, Sheldon and Irma met with the doctor, he pronounced Sheldon medically qualified for the surgical implant, opened the brochure of replacement models, and inquired as to Sheldon's and Irma's choice. "Frankly, Doctor," Irma said, "we'd rather put the money into a new kitchen."

2.01 Schmuck

Everyone, except the *schmuck* himself, usually knows what a *schmuck* is. (We had a colleague—a real *schmuck*—who was wont to follow us around and ask, "Why am I a *schmuck*? Why am I a *schmuck* . . . ?"[4]) *Schmuck* can also be used as a hortatory expletive, to try to wake a *schmuck* from his state of *schmuckdom*. In a pan-religious historical example that incorporates both usages, and which Sol Farblondget uses as prologue to *The World According to Schmucks*, we can infer the vast sway of this form of *minor mishegas*, and sense its omnipresence through the ages.

Once upon a time, to determine the nature of the One True God (or the Three-in-One God), Jesus and Moses met on the shores of the Red Sea, where their followers had gathered by the thousands. Recently circumcised on his eighth day of life at an extravagant 'destination *bris*,' a cherubic infant who would become the *chochem gadol* (great wise man) known

---

4 What a *schmuck*!

as 'The Two Thousand Year Old Man' (but 'The One Thousand Nine Hundred and Ninety Eight Year Old Man' to close friends and associates), then in his original incarnation as 'The Nine Day Old *Bondit*,' was chosen to judge the event, in which Moses and Jesus would see who could walk on water. "There can only be one winner, fellas," the Nine Day Old *Bondit* declared. "So tough titty on everyone else."

And so, in his long white robe, and carrying a large wooden crucifix his mother Mary had thoughtfully coated with *shmalz* to protect it from wind, rain, and pigeon poop, Jesus stepped into the shallows of the Red Sea. And then, looking more like Charlton Heston than ever—carrying a blue velvet-covered Torah in his arms, its silver-laden spindles and breast plate gleaming in the sun—Moses stepped into the Red Sea. The Children of Israel rejoiced in song and prayer, and the Christians did the same. The music of "*Hava Negilah*" and Latin chants filled the air as the two great men strode forward, side by side, water lapping at the hems of their robes.

A minute or so later, the water rose to Moses's ankles, and then to his calves, while Jesus strode forward proudly on the sea's rippled surface. Side by side, the two men moved ahead, with Moses sinking lower and lower—the water rising to his waist, to his chest, to his throat—and so the Jews began to weep and tear at their hair while the Christians sang a rapturous song of thanksgiving: "This land is *my* land . . . this land is *my* land . . . !"

Moses held the Torah above his head even as the water rose to his mouth, and then to his nose. With sorrowful eyes, he looked up toward the heavens.

"Why, God?" he cried. "Why me?"

To which God gave the traditional answer: "Why *not* you?" And then, in a whisper: "*Schmuck*—do what my son is doing—walk on the rocks!"

In more recent times, a different Moses—Moses Cheppeh, a senior citizen living in Del Ray Beach, Florida—decided to make repairs on his house, and his friend Moredcai offered to help.

On the first day Moses gave Mordecai a hammer and a box of nails, then went off to get more lumber and some shingles for the roof. When he returned he saw Mordecai sitting on a stool, hundreds of bent nails around his feet. Moses watched as Mordecai kept putting the flat ends of the nails against the wood, then hammering at the pointed ends.

"*Shmuck*!" he said to Mordecai. "Those nails are for the *other* side of the house!"

2.02 Schlemiel

A *schlemiel* should never be confused with a *schmuck*. A *schlemiel* is an essentially stupid inept, submissive, and ineffectual man[5] to whom unlucky

---

5 In a familiar instance, Herbie Krichmar comes home from Hebrew School with the good news that he has a part in the Passover play. "And what part will you be playing?" Herbie's mother asks. "The father!" Herbie says proudly. "Too bad," the mother says. "I was hoping maybe you'd get a speaking part."

things happen. "The *schlemiel* falls on his back," clinical studies demonstrate, "and breaks his nose." A *schlemiel* is pathologically incapable of doing things right and should not be confused with his close cousin, the *nebish*. (A *schlemiel* knocks a glass of prune juice off a table; the *nebish* wipes it up.)

Nor should a *schlemiel* be confused with a *schlemazel*.

2.03 Schlemazel

A *schlemazel*, typically, has hot borscht spilled down his neck by a *schlemiel*. A *schlemazel* is a chronically unlucky human being, and physicians through the ages have drawn on traditional folk sayings, many collected by the great scholar of Yiddish lexicology, Leo Rosten, to explain the *schlemazel*'s haplessness: "When a *schlemazel* winds a clock, it stops; when he kills a chicken, it walks; when he sells umbrellas, the sun comes out; and when he manufactures shrouds, people stop dying."

2.04 Schmegegge

A true *schmegegge* can be recognized by the pleasure people take in articulating (with disdain) this wonderful onomatopoetic term to describe a person who is part *schlemiel*, part *schlemazel*, and a whining sycophant to boot. Your brother-in-law usually qualifies as a *schmegegge*. Or if he's the successful one, it's you who is the *schmegegge*.

2.05 Schmendrick

A *schmendrik* is a kind of *schlemiel*-in-training, but with this difference: he *thinks* he can succeed, and becomes more *schlemiel*-like than the most inept *schlemiel* by his ill-advised attempts. Thus, Yossel Paskudnyak, turned down for membership in an exclusive WASP country club, asked his friend, Winthrop Warren Wellington Whitney Wembley III & IV, to help him. "Here's my idea — you sponsor me under an alias, they accept me, and *then* I inform them of who I really am, so that they risk humiliating publicity and major law suits if they reverse their decision and try to throw me out."

Winthrop Wellington Warren Whitney Wembley III & IV gave Yossel an application form, which Yossel filled out and sent in. Two weeks later, Yossel stormed into the law office of Winthrop Wembley Warren Wellington Whitney III & IV, on fire with the news that he had been rejected yet again by the country club.

Winthrop Warren Whitney Wembley Wellington III & IV, who never raised his voice or perspired, asked Yossel some questions.

"What name did you give — not Yossel Paskudnyak?"

"Of course not. I gave my name as James Henry Hardy Hamilton."

"And profession — you didn't put 'tailor?'"

"I put down 'venture capitalist.'"

"And for religion — you didn't put down 'Jew,' did you?"

"Of course not," Yossel said. "I put down '*goy*.'"

2.06. Schnook, Schmo, Schlub, Yutz, Putz

Although the *mayvens* who continue to author the ever-changing thousand-page *D.S.M.* might make uselessly subtle distinctions between the above named diagnostic categories included in *cockamammy conditions of character*, to do so would be like trying to count the number of *putzes* dancing on the roof of Heshy Farkas's lovingly restored 1951 Buick Roadmaster on the occasion of his third divorce from his wife Marla (who, by the time of her seventh divorce and eighth marriage, we are told, had permanent rice marks on her face).

Shnooks, shmos, shlubs, and most *putzes* are generally nincompoops and *yutzes* (clueless, annoying, socially inept individuals) who are easily fooled and taken advantage of. Gullible and incompetent, they compensate for their deficiencies by being submissive to overbearing men and nagging wives. As husbands, though, they always have the last word ("Yes, dear"); as friends they are born losers ("You'll let me loan you my car *and* girlfriend for the weekend if I promise to pay for the gas? Gee—what a deal . . . !"). Their ability to persist in their foolishness, though admirable, is usually self-defeating.

Thus, Avie Schiffenbauer, who made *aliyah* to Israel shortly after his second wife left him for their synagogue's third assistant rabbi, spent the remainder of his life praying at The Wailing Wall. When we visited him there recently, we asked him how many years it had been, and how often he prayed.

"Oh, I been praying here three times every day for 39 years now, and on Shabbos and all the holidays too, come rain or come shine or large groups of Hadassah women."

"And in all these years," we asked, "what did you pray for?"

"I prayed that children shouldn't go hungry," Avie said. "I prayed that Jews and Palestinians should, like the lion and the lamb, lie down beside one another. I prayed for an end to disease, pestilence, tsunamis, tornadoes, reality TV shows, and floods. And most of all I prayed for world peace."

"And do you think, in all these years, that your prayers have been answered?" we asked.

Whereupon Avie rolled his eyes, and shook his head sideways. "Whaddaya mean, have my prayers been answered," he said. "It's like talking to a wall!"

2.07 Shnorrer

A *shnorrer* is a beggar, a cheapskate, a moocher. In the *shtetl* of Shtiklech, Leibish Geshmat was a well-known *shnorrer*. One day, unable to get to the other side of the street quickly enough, he was stopped by Izzie Pareve, who asked if Leibish remembered that Izzie had loaned him 50 rubles many months before.

"Of course I remember," Leibish said.

"And do you remember that you promised to pay me back?" Izzie asked.

"Of course I remember," Leibish said.

"So I was wondering if maybe you could tell me *when* you expect to pay me back?" Izzie asked.

"Am I a prophet?" Leibish replied.

2.08 Kvetch

To complain in a whiney often high-pitched tone. *Kvetch* can also be used as a noun, to refer to the person who *kvetches* (and is therefore a *kvetch* or *kvetcher*). In their eternal insatiability, *kvetchers* have many affinities with *tsuris*-addicts. For example, when Tillie Kwestel's grandson, Morton, was swept out to sea on a beach in Boca Raton, she cried out to God with great gusto that He should bring her little Morton back from death at once. Her non-stop *kvetching* was answered a few minutes later when, with a gigantic whoosh, a large wave threw her grandson up on the sand. Tillie took Morton in her arms, smoothed down his hair and then, indignantly, hands on hips, looked up at the sky. "When he went in," she said, "he was wearing a baseball cap."

2.09 Noodj

Noodj, too, can be both a verb (to *noodj* somebody) or a noun (to be one who *noodjs* others). To *noodj* is to nag, pester, and keep after someone relentlessly to do what you want them to do. The general plaint of someone who makes others suffer from this ailment is 'I-want-what-I-want-when-I-want-it-and-I-won't stop-*hocking*-you-until-I-get-it.'

For example, in The Holy Land, Boruch Halevai, a man tired of life, goes into the desert and cries out to God: "Oh Lord, I have been a good and honest man. I have never cheated anyone in my business dealings. I have been faithful to my wife, good to my children and grandchildren, and honorable to my friends and relatives. I have prayed three times a day ever since my Bar Mitzvah. I have given more than generously to charity . . . and yet my business fails, my health declines, my children and grandchildren are rude to me, my wife has stopped sleeping with me, my friends spurn me, my stomach bothers me, my flatulence is ungovernable and drives away customers, and in the meantime, my neighbor, Mendel Kippis, who cheats in business, and cheats on his wife, and steals from the charity box, and never goes to *schul* — this *momzer* (see **Cockamamy Conditions of Character 2.11**) prospers. So tell me, God, why does he prosper while I have nothing but misfortune? Why does he become rich while I become poorer and poorer? Why, God, does a good, believing, faithful man like myself know nothing but misery? *Why, God? Why? Why? Why?*"

Weeping away, and tearing at his ragged poncho, Boruch throws himself on the desert floor, at which point the clouds part, a bolt of lightning streaks across the sky, a deafening clap of thunder booms through the heavens, and God's voice is heard.

"*Why?*" God says. "Because you *noodj* me too much, that's why!"

2.10 Yenta

A *yenta* is a blabbermouth — a person who thrives on gossip and spreading gossip, and is constitutionally unable to keep her mouth shut, keep a secret, or respect a confidence.[6]

An illustrative instance: Four women are playing canasta, as they do every Wednesday afternoon. "You know, ladies," Pearl says, "I have known you all for a very long time, and there's something I've got to get off my chest. I am a kleptomaniac. But don't get excited — I've never stolen from any of you and I never will." Ethel plays a card, then speaks: "Well, since we're into true confessions today, I can confide in you that I am a practicing nymphomaniac, but I want to assure you that I never slept with any of your husbands and I never will." Evelyn says that she also has a confession to make. "The reason I never married," she says, "is that I'm a lesbian, but I wouldn't want to endanger our friendship so I will never, ever hit on any of you." At this point, Fanny pushes herself away from the table and stands. "Ladies, I too have a confession to make," she says. "I'm a *yenta*, so please excuse me because I have a lot of calls to make."

---

6 This diagnostic category is usually reserved for women; when a man — an arrogant lawyer, a TV anchor, a shoe salesman — has these qualities, he is called 'a real *balmalocha*' — a *yenta-with-facts*.

2.11 Momzer

A *momzer* — literally, a bastard — refers to any mean-spirited, nasty, untrustworthy, unscrupulous, detestable man. A *momzer* should not be confused with a *no-goodnik* or a *gonif*, both of whom may be forgiven their *mishegas*. While true *momzers* are relatively rare, *no-goodniks* and *gonifs* abound. A *no-goodnik* is not a serious danger to others — mildly dishonest rather than cruel or psychopathic, and can be identified by his parents' lament that from him they will never get *nachas*. A *gonif* is, literally, a thief or a crook, and the term can be used metaphorically, as in "That *gonif* stole my heart and stomped on it and didn't even leave a return address!" But it can also be a term of endearment, as when a grandparent, seeing a grandchild sneaking a halvah bar from the pantry, exclaims with delight, "Oh what a little *gonif* that *bubula* is!"

One cannot say that a *momzer* truly suffers from *mishegas* for this would imply that *momzers* are victims. But a *momzer* spends his life victimizing *others*, and is a victim, if at all, due only to his innate pathological nature. When a *momzer* is also a *macher* (a big shot), the combination is deadly.

For example, one Yom Kippur — the Jewish Day of Atonement and Holiest Day of the Year — Seymour Shlockmeister, who had made fortunes in the real estate business by block-busting neighborhoods to rid them of blacks and immigrants, by foreclosing on widows and disabled tour guides, and by successfully bribing any banking and government official he could, decides to play golf on a day when, at the Jewish Country Club to which he belongs, the course is deserted.

Sitting on fluffy autumnal clouds, Sid Gruber and Herman Feldstein, brought to ruin and early graves by the ways Shlockmeister drove them out of business, are looking down from heaven. They are reminiscing about their wives, their children, their grandchildren, their friends, and talking about what they wouldn't do for a good toasted bagel with lox and a healthy *shmeer* of cream cheese, when they spot Shlockmeister on the golf course. They shake their heads in disgust as Shlockmeister tees off on the first hole — at 475 yards, the longest fairway in the world — and the ball sails through the air, bounces twice, and goes *kerplunk!* into the cup for a hole-in-one.

"With luck like that," Sid says, "small wonder that *momzer* of *momzers* gets away with murder his whole life long. There he is, thumbing his nose at God, and at Jews everywhere who are in *shul* and fasting, and look at him, doing what even Tiger Woods has never done . . . "

To these words, Herman smiles a smile of heavenly bliss. "Ah yes, Sid, but look at it this way — who can he tell?"

2.12 Chalaria

A *chalaria*, in her way, is the female equivalent of a *momzer*: a shrew, a witch, a bitch, though rarely a destructive force (unless you're married to her). A *chalaria* is a woman who carries on . . . and on . . . and on . . . . Famed in the Old Country as '*La Belle Dame Sans Merci*-and-*Pas De Quoi*,' *chalarias* have been tormenting men, women, children, old people, and small domestic animals for centuries.

For example, a *chalaria* is the person who, at a *bris*, shouts out, "Are you sure you cut off enough?" And at a wedding, when the young couple is under the wedding canopy, a *chalaria* will call out that they shouldn't worry because if things don't work out, they can always get a divorce. And if people try to shush her, she will only become more agitated and shout that it is her *responsibility* to let these children know that the reason divorces can cost even more than weddings is because they're worth it. At the reception afterwards, when the assembled guests are toasting the newlyweds with champagne, she will announce that the reason she is not drinking today is because it interferes with her suffering. "And remember this," she will tell the bridegroom. "A bad wife is worse than death." And if the bridegroom asks why, she will answer, "Because death only comes once." [7]

---

7 Most people wish that *chalarias*, like *momzers*, should die often and painfully, but according to our research, this happens only occasionally. When dealing with *chalarias*, Sol Farblondget recommends reminding yourself of an adage that has served him well through the years: that a fool can throw a stone into the water that ten wise men cannot recover. And when it comes to *chalarias* and *momzers*, a corollary: that if *chalarias* and *momzers* are afflicted with kidney stones that cannot be recovered, that's fine too.

2.13 Alrightnik (masculine), Alrightnikeh (feminine)

An *alrightnik* is *not* the opposite of a *no-goodnik*. In fact, *alrightniks* and *no-goodniks* have much in common, especially the fact that both are, to employ current psychoanalytically informed terminology, stinking low-life bums. The difference is that *alrightniks* think their armpits don't stink: they compound whatever small success may come their way with arrogance and stupidity. Thus, an *alrightnik*'s wife, saved from drowning on a beach in Far Rockaway, is surrounded by bathers. "Call a doctor!" people cry. "Dial 911 . . . ! Give her artificial respiration!"

"Never!" says the *alrightnik*. "*Real* respiration or nothing!"

And when Murray Garmentovich, famed for selling cheap knock-offs of clothing from Gucci, Armani, and K-Mart, entered Mount Sinai Hospital on a recent morning, he did so in top hat, white tie, and tails. Tired of having little Garmentoviches keep his wife from giving him the adoration he craved, he was at Mount Sinai for a vasectomy. The Intake Nurse took Murray's insurance cards, verified the schedule for surgery, gave him his wrist bands, privacy statement, and room number, and then, as he was sauntering out of the office, said that she could not help but wonder why he was dressed in such formal attire.

"Listen, baby doll," Murray said. "If you're gonna be impotent, you gotta look impotent."

3.0 Categories Of Mishegas Relating To Food, Sex, And Age

As we move into our golden years, and have more time for the essentials of life—food and sex—we also come to enjoy them *and* to worry about them in increasingly *ferkachta* (screwy, mixed up) ways. In an example Sol Farblondget experienced first-hand when visiting his brother-in-law Menachem Uberpisher, who was recovering from surgery in a Fort Lauderdale hospital, we can see how these three elements can be joined.

Sol's sister, Faygelah, who picked Sol up at the airport, said that while he visited with Menachem she would have her hair done and get on line so they could be seated at an early bird special without having to wait an hour for a table.

At the hospital, Menachem told him the story. "Just between us," Menachem said, "here's what happened. My friend Shimmy Trombenik, a widower for three years already, told me about a woman he met on the beach. They got to talking, she invited him to her apartment, asked if he would like some dessert, and when he said yes, she clapped her hands in delight. 'Oh do I have a surprise for you!' she said, after which she undressed him, massaged his body with fragrant oils and, on his rising member, put a doughnut, a scoop ice cream, some whipped cream, chopped nuts, a cherry, a large spoonful of hot butterscotch sauce—his favorite—and then began slowly nibbling at her concoction.

The woman told Menachem she had decided this was the perfect senior citizen leisure-time activity, for despite the calories, her body was staying wonderfully fit and her digestive tract in the best working order of her life. And if Shimmy had any friends he could recommend, she would be happy to share dessert with them too.

"I declined the offer of course — I love your sister the way I love my own wife — " Menachem said " — but Shimmy kept insisting I try it once, and finally I said, okay, okay already. So I went to her apartment, and it was like he said — the undressing, the massage, and — for me — a bagel, a healthy *shmeer* cream cheese, some lox, a sliced onion . . . "

At this point Menachem began crying softly, lifted the sheet that was covering him, and showed Sol the bandage covering his private parts.

"It looked so good," Menachem said, "I took a bite myself."

3.01 Alter Kocker (A.K.)

An *alter kocker, or A.K.,* is an old fart, and the designation can sometimes be used self-referentially to rationalize behavior, as in: "So I put the dog food in the coffee grinder and peed on the floor again, but what can I do? I'm an *alter kocker!*"

The *D.S.M.* sets forth dozens of categories to tell you what you already know about a simple, natural fact of life: that if we live long enough, we all become forgetful *alter kockers.*

But so what? If you're an *alter kocker,* you're an *alter kocker*, and you don't need some scientific sounding nonsense about cognitive deficits and impairments not otherwise specified except when driving with a broken axle one or two in the wrong lane with physiological and neurological explanations notwithstanding or disturbing other drivers who have their own etiologies and prostates to worry about. "The truth," Sol Farblondget has often said, "is that being an *alter kocker* ain't such a bad thing, especially if you compare it to being a teenager."

As with all other essentials of life, natural and unnatural (marriage, sex, circumcision, sex, food, sex, food, work, sex, food, in-laws, sex, food, death, sex, food, shuffleboard, sex, and food), there are ways to see the bad news in *alter kockerdom* . . . or the good news. Thus, when 80 year old Nachman Meisner asked his friend, 81 year old Nathan Gluckstern, how he could have married 82 year old Gittel Lebovsky, who was fat, ugly, ill-mannered, sexless, and a bad cook, Nathan nodded at the recitation of each item. "True—all true," he said.

"So why did you marry her?" Nachman asked.

"She can drive at night," Nathan said.

Or take this example, which appears in a "*Mayvens of Mishegas*" anthology that has become a staple of couples therapy: *Sex after Seventy: Rising to the Occasion and Coming Together*.[8a]

8a When Ruth Sharopnikel, a widow, read the book, she immediately went to her friend Anat Tsatske's apartment. "What it says in the book," she told Anat, who was also a widow, "is

On a beautiful spring day, Babalu Greenberg sees his lifelong friend Alvin Putzelovich, sitting on a bench in Central Park, where they have met daily since they retired a dozen years before. Alvin, head in hands, is weeping. Babalu puts his arm around Alvin, and asks him what the matter is.

Alvin tells him he met a wonderful young woman, Adriana Courtney Simpson Shapiro, and they began having coffee together, the famous one thing led to another, and Adriana fell madly in love with Alvin. She moved in with him, and she made love to him every morning before she left for work (she was a part-time fashion model and full-time licensed plumber), and she came home mid-day, Monday to Friday, to bring him lunch and perform oral sex on him. In the evenings she made elegant candle-lit dinners, played pinochle with him, and before sleep, very very slowly, she made love to him again.

At this point, Alvin began blubbering, his body wracked with sobs, and Babalu said that it all sounded incredibly wonderful, and he was happy for his friend's good fortune, so why was he so upset?

"I can't remember where I live!" Alvin cried, and burst into tears again.

---

that the very best thing you can have with your husband is mutual orgasm." "Who knew?" Anat replied, to which Ruth asked if when Anat's husband, Abe, was alive, they ever had mutual orgasm. Anat thought for a minute, then shook her head. "I think we had All-State," she said.

3.02 Dementia With Benefits

As we have seen with *Nervous Conditions of Everyday Life* and *Cockamamy Conditions of Character*, many forms of *mishegas*, including incipient dementias, can be transformed from liabilities into assets. For example, a retired couple, Jake and Sadie, determined to head off dementia by following the Surgeon General's recommendations for seniors — to exercise regularly and develop new interests — made an appointment to see a sex therapist, and when the therapist asked them why they were there, they said they would like him to observe them while in the act of making love. The therapist said he had done this for other couples, and told them to proceed.

So Jake and Sadie took off one another's clothes, and they made love. When they were done, and had their clothes back on, the therapist asked them how they felt.

"Terrific," Jake said.

"Wonderful," Sadie said.

The therapist said he did not observe anything of concern — that they seemed quite compatible. Jake and Sadie thanked the therapist, and asked if he could see them again the following week.

The therapist agreed. When they arrived the next time, they again asked if the therapist would observe them while they made love. He did, and when they were done and dressed, they talked again of how pleasurable the love-making was, and the therapist again told them he saw no areas of concern, and yes, he would be willing to see them the following week.

When the same thing happened two more times, the therapist said that since they had no sexual problems, or emotional problems connected to sex, he wondered why they continued to come to his office.

"Well, the truth is, I'm married," Jake said, "so we can't do it in my apartment."

"And I'm married too," Sadie said, "so we can't do it in my apartment."

"And if we go to a Howard Johnson's, it's a hundred and fifty dollars," Jake explained.

"But if we come here," Sadie said, "Medicare and AARP cover the whole thing."

As Sol points out, especially for single men and women, the years when dementias begin to arrive, and you begin to forget all the *tsuris* you've been through, can be the best years of your life. Without a day job, without children at home, and — statistics don't lie — especially if you are spouse-free, life can be filled with adventure, sex, and romance. But for this to happen, Sol suggests that you be enterprising in the pursuit of your pleasures.

Take, for example, Harold Krochmal, a hard-working piece-goods finisher who had a loving relationship with his wife Pauline of 53 years until she passed away at the age of 75. So Harold retired to an assisted living community in White Plains, New

---

8 Sick?

York, and on his first day there, noticing that men were greatly outnumbered by women, he tacked an index card to the bulletin board outside the communal dining room:

Had enough of intimacy? For earthly delights with a warm, vital man, come to Apartment 36J

Early the next morning, a lovely gray-haired woman appeared at Harold's door. "How much?" she asked.

Harold was impressed by the woman's directness, and responded in kind: "Five dollars for the floor," he said, "ten dollars for the couch, twenty dollars for the bedroom."

The woman reached into her pocket book, took out a twenty dollar bill.

"This way, please," Harold said, closing the door behind them, and heading for the bedroom.

The woman grabbed Harold's arm. "Oh no you don't!" she said, holding the twenty dollar bill high in the air while pointing at Herbie's feet. "Four times on the floor!"

But it's not only single men and women who can have dementia-with-benefits. Take a couple like Frieda Plotnick and Fred Plotstein, who went to their local CVS pharmacy and asked to see the manager. He appeared, and they took out a list and began asking questions: Did his store carry hearing aids? Reading glasses? Canes? Walkers? Blood pressure cuffs? Epsom salts? Viagra? Personal female lubricants? Diapers? Geritol?

The manager said yes to each item.

"Terrific," Fred said, and shook the manager's hand vigorously. *"Mazel Tov! Mazel Tov!"*

"I don't understand," the manager said.

"We're getting married," Frieda explained, "and we'd like to use your store for our Wedding Registry."

3.03 Fressers

A *fresser* (from the verb *to fress*) can never eat enough. Thus, Shirley, a habitual *fresser*, visits her neighbor Lois while Lois is baking oatmeal raisin cookies for her grandchildren. "They smell wonderful," Shirley says, and asks if Lois minds if she tastes one. "Please," Lois says. A while later, Shirley, who is meanwhile *noshing* liberally on all the other food Lois puts out—chopped liver, humus, cheese, crackers, nuts, raisins, dried prunes, olives, gherkins, herring rolls —says that the cookies are so good, she is wondering if she can have another. "Please," Lois says, and Shirley eats another.

A half hour later, Shirley says, "I know I've already had four cookies, but could I have just one more?"

"You've already had five," Lois replies, "but who's counting?"

3.04 Chazzer

A *chazzer* is, by literal definition, a pig. A *chazzer* can't stop stuffing himself or herself with food, and in a *farpotshket* (messy) manner. Even on their deathbeds, *chazzers* are still *chazzers*. Thus, when Hymie Flayshedik, in a coma and dying, smelled one of his favorite foods—appropriately enough, pigs-in-a-blanket (small hot dogs in pastry puffs)—he pushed away his covers, fell out of bed and, following the aroma, crawled to the staircase and tumbled down the stairs into the kitchen, where his wife was taking a tray of pigs-in-a-blanket out of the oven.

Hymie got to his knees, and reached up to the counter, where a tray of pigs-in-a-blanket was cooling, at which point his wife whacked him on the hand with a wooden spoon.

"Those are for *after* the funeral," she said.

3.05 Mishugener Eating Categories Not Elsewhere Classified

In addition to well-known, primitive eating rituals such as all-you-can eat buffets, or cannibalism (where practitioners have been known to pass their mothers in the forest), Sol Farblondget, in a psychologically compelling tale of unrequired [sic][8] love, provides a memorable example of the miraculous, incomprehensible, and paradoxical quality of human nature, and of how sex, food, and religious traditions can sometimes be strangely and mysteriously joined.

Rabbi Shmuel Kanutopdiss owned a *glatt* kosher bakery and delicatessen in the Catskills. He was an observant Jew who complied with all Jewish laws, thus the designation *glatt*, which assured the Jewish community that he was adhering to all rabbinic regulations, especially *kashruth*: the rules governing food that separated what was kosher ('clean,' and therefore edible) from what was *treyf* ('unclean,' and therefore forbidden). Pious Jews came from far and wide to buy his bread, and to *nosh* overpriced and tasteless food in the small tea room and delicatessen that adjoined his bakery.

His eldest son, Joshua, delivered bread six days a week to both kosher and non-kosher restaurants in the surrounding counties. One day while Joshua was in the kitchen of the Basta-Pasta Hotel, which had a mostly Italian clientele, delivering several sacks of bread, he heard alarming huffing, puffing, and moaning sounds.

He set down the sacks of bread, hurried past the stoves and the pantry, and there on the floor was his father-the-*rebbe*, bare-assed, and with his *tsitsis* (fringed undergarment) and *shtreimel* (furred hat) lying beside him, and the wife of the hotel's owner, Gabriela Garibaldi Garibaldi, lying under him while he *shtupped* her with abandon. (*Shtup:* to push, to press, to fornicate.)

Joshua was aghast. "*Poppa, Poppa!*" he cried out. "*Is it really you?*"

"Yes," his father replied. "But it's all right—I don't eat here."

3.06 Shikker

A *shikker* is a drunkard, and is not to be confused with a *shiksa* — a non-Jewish girl and, thus, a curseword to many Jewish parents.[9] To a *shikker* the only thing worse than drink is thirst. Thus, when Rose Kreplach was at her wit's end because her husband Saul was coming home drunk every night, she went down to the neighborhood bar where she knew he spent his evenings.

When Saul saw her, he smiled with delight, introduced her to his friends, and invited her to have a drink with him.

"Never! I want you to stop. I want you to stop, Saul!" Rose said, at which point Saul pointed to his friend Bernie, who had just keeled over face-first *splat!* onto the floor.

"That's Bernie for you," Saul said. "He always knows when to stop."

Rose kept begging Saul to stop drinking, and he kept inviting her to have a drink, and when he

---

9 When Arnie Finkelstein brought home his bride, a Native American (and *shiksa*), and introduced her to his mother — 'Momma, this is Running Deer' — his mother replied, "If you're Running Deer, then I'm 'Sitting Shiva,'" and slammed the door in her son's face, after which she and her husband chanted *Kaddish*, and began announcing to one and all that their son was dead to them. One evening, five years later, Arnie's mother answered the phone, and it was her son calling and begging her not to hang up because he had wonderful news for them. They were the grandparents of a beautiful baby boy! What's more, Arnie and his wife had decided to give their son a Jewish name! The mother asked what her grandson's name was. "We're calling him Little White Fish," Arnie said.

promised that if she did, he would go home with her, Rose agreed.

The bartender poured her a glass *schnapps*. She drank it, gagged, and nearly spit it all out.

"Why this stuff is awful!" she said.

"See?" Saul said. "And here you're thinking I'm down here having a good time every night!"

3.07 Farshlepteh Krenk

Farshlepteh Krenk is the Yiddish diagnostic term for a condition similar to hypochondria. In an illustrative paradigm, a Frenchman, an Irishman, and a Jew walk into a bar.

"I'm tired and thirsty," says the Frenchman. "I must have wine."

"I'm tired and thirsty," says the Irishman. "I must have beer."

"I'm tired and thirsty," says the Jew. "I must have diabetes."

4.0 Appendix[10] Relating To Ethics And Matters Otherwise Unspecified

Unlike the *D.S.M.*, which piles up thousands of diagnoses and distinctions without ever talking about a real human being, we have done our best

10 The appendix can, of course, upon accurate diagnosis, be removed.

to put many of the infinite varieties of *mishegas* into human contexts. Although we are sensitive to the moral implications of being *mishugah* and dealing with *mishugeners*, for us to consider such weighty ethical matters here would, for starters, require a *megillah* (a long tale; a boring treatise) twice as long as what we have already given you, and would drive up the price of our book in a way guaranteed to kill sales.

But to give readers a sense of what a discussion of '*Mishegas* and Morality' might be like, we cite the story of a father explaining ethics to his son.

"Now let's say a woman comes in and orders a hundred dollars worth of material," the father says. "You wrap it up, and you give it to her. She pays you with a $100 bill. But as she is leaving, you realize she has given you *two* $100 bills. Now here, you see, is where ethics come in: Should you or should you not tell your partner?"

In surveying the basics of *mishegas*, we have, of course, only skimmed the surface of the multitude of ways in which human beings are *mishugah* and drive each other *mishugah*. We have chosen not to include genuine physical and neurological diseases of the brain that can bring on categories of *mishegas* because they are so numerous they would require their own manual.[11] For example, *loch in kop* (literally, a hole in the head, but often employed as a means of *de*-tachment, as in screaming at someone: "I need you like I need a *loch in kop!*"), or traumatizing head

---

11 In progress!

Jay Neugeboren, Michael B. Friedman, Lloyd I. Sederer M.D.

injuries brought on by excessive exposure to *kvetch-ing* and *hocking*, when victims are known to cry out in their distress, *"Hock nit kain chainik!"* — literally, "Don't hit the teapot."

When attempting to alleviate such disabling conditions, however, we recommend keeping in mind Sol Farblondget's maxim and unfailing panacea — that a Selective Serotonin Re-uptake Inhibitor is no substitute for a good piece herring.

Also: we have left out many disorders — e.g., *pisher, luftmensch, neatnik, nudnik, klutz, shvitzer, shlump, dumkopf,* etc. — that seemed to us so common as to be beneath inclusion in a manual dedicated to eschewing any form of evidence or scientific standards, thereby holding fast to Sol's commonsensical criteria and totally insane enterprise.

But who knows? Maybe if we live long enough and, along with testimonials to the more enlightened levels of *mishegas* to which our manual has taken you — and if you will be kind enough to send us your corrections, additions, subtractions, and stories — we'll someday put out a revised edition of our manual the way the people who revise the *D.S.M.* do every few years (so that every health care worker in America has to throw out their old *D.S.M.* and buy the new one for over a hundred bucks) . . .

. . . Except that our promise is that we will make sure any revision of *The Diagnostic Manual of Mishegas* is even thinner and — is such a thing possible? — *more* useful than it already is!

61

"Love is sweet," Sol Farblondget tells couples who come to him for guidance, "but tastes best with bread."

And oh boy, does Sol love bread! [12] What he understands is that we're all a little bit *mishugah*, and that's just fine, because most kinds of *mishegas* — like love! — make the world go round, which is why, as Mister Shakespeare wrote in the original and unexpurgated version of his play, *A Midsummer Night's Driml*, "the lunatic, the lover, and the poet are of imagination and *mishegas* all compact."

---

[12] Sol's favorite, combining as it does both romance and *mishegas*, is, of course, date-nut bread.